Professor Bumblebrain's Bonkers Book on...

PARABLES

Published 2013 by CWR, Waverley Abbey House, Waverley Lane, Farnham, Surrey GU9 8EP, England.
CWR is a Registered Charity - Number 294387 and a Limited Company registered in England -
Registartion Number 1990308.

See back of book for list of National Distributors.
Editing, design and production by CWR
Printed in Croatia by Zrinski
ISBN: 978-1-85345-947-4

Professor Bumblebrain's Bonkers Book on...

PARABLES

ANDY ROBB

CWR

What is a parable you may ask?

MEOW! MEOW! MEOW!

Precisely, Einstein! My faithful cat has answered the question perfectly. He says that parables are stories Jesus told to help people understand what God is like and how He wants us to live.

I'D HAVE SAID THAT MYSELF BUT PROFESSOR BUMBLEBRAIN PREFERS IT IF I ONLY SPEAK IN CAT LANGUAGE.

The Gospels bit of the Bible is brimming over with Jesus' parables which people jostled to hear as He went from place to place speaking about God to the crowds.

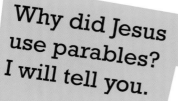

Why did Jesus use parables? I will tell you.

IT ISN'T ALWAYS EASY TO GET OUR HEADS AROUND THINGS TO DO WITH GOD, EVEN WHEN YOU HAVE A BRAIN THE SIZE OF A LARGE CABBAGE LIKE I DO.

That's because God is in heaven and we are on the earth. Heaven is altogether different from this world but God's plan is for as many as possible of the good things of heaven to come down to earth.

Professor Bumblebrain's Information Station:
Heaven is absolutely perfect and there's not a jot of
badness to be found there, try as you might to find it.

NOT EVEN JUST A TEENSY BIT OF BADNESS?

STOP, THIEF!

No, not even a teensy bit! So, for those of us who want to have a bash at doing things on earth the way they are done in heaven the parables are there to show us how to go about it.

I'D BETTER GIVE IT A GO THEN, HADN'T I?

Yes, indeed!

Here's the thing. In heaven, God runs the show and everyone does what God says. Not because they have to but because they want to.

God's a good God so falling in line with Him is a no-brainer. Because everyone in heaven does things God's way, everything is wonderful. Not so on Planet Earth. Although the world was in tip-top condition when God created it, it didn't stay that way for long. People soon chose to do things their way and not God's way which is why there's so much bad stuff around.

ARE YOU HAVING A DIG AT ME?

The Bible (a book about God) calls anywhere that God is allowed to rule and reign, the kingdom of God.

The parables were Jesus' way of showing us how we could experience the kingdom of God here on the earth.

MEOW! MEOW!

Some of the seed fell along the road and was quickly gobbled up by a bunch of hungry birds.

Some of the seed landed on rocky ground.
Because the soil wasn't very deep it shot up in no time.

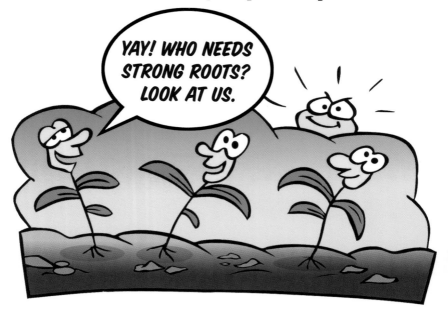

Some of the seed landed slap bang in a clump of thorn bushes and got choked to death.

UUUGH! YOU ROTTER!

But the good news is that some seed fell on fertile soil where it sprung to life producing a humongous harvest.

YOU'LL WHAT PROFESSOR?

Oh, I forgot that not everyone has the very vast and varied vocabulary that I do. Elucidate means to explain clearly. Got that? Good! Now where were we?

The seeds that fell on good ground represent people who welcome what God has to say with open arms. When you do that it's like a bumper crop of God's goodness growing up inside of you.

The religious leaders thought that by keeping a whole bunch of rules and regulations they were better than everyone else.

They'd lost the plot big time.

God was never into rules for rules' sake.

Our relationship with God and how we treat our neighbours (other people) has always been top of God's to-do list.

YES, BUT WHO IS OUR NEIGHBOUR? TELL ME THAT!

First up, a Jewish priest walked by. Did he lend the trounced traveller a helping hand?

I'm afraid not. He swiftly passed by on the other side of the road.

Next up, along came a Levite (a guy who served in Jerusalem's Temple). Guess what? He did the very same thing and also walked by on the other side of the road.

... rocked up. Just for your information, when it came to the Jews and Samaritans there wasn't a lot of love lost between them, so it would have been a big surprise to Jesus' listeners when He announced that it was the Samaritan who actually stopped to help the injured Jew.

The Samaritan not only bandaged up the man's wounds but transported him on his donkey to an inn to rest until the poor chap was better. To add to his kindness the Samaritan even paid the innkeeper for his trouble.

Jesus rounded off the parable by asking His audience who *they* thought was a real neighbour to the injured man. Was it those two fellas who kept all their religious rules and regulations but didn't lift a finger to help?

Or was it the Samaritan?

THE ONE WHO SHOWED PITY.

GO AND DO THE SAME!

Not all the parables that Jesus told were quite so straightforward.

Some were very puzzling indeed and I would imagine it wasn't only the religious leaders who were left scratching their heads and wondering what on earth He was talking about.

TOO RIGHT! JESUS SAID THAT THE KINGDOM OF HEAVEN IS LIKE SOMEONE DISCOVERING SOME BURIED TREASURE IN A FIELD, QUICKLY COVERING IT UP AGAIN THEN SELLING EVERYTHING THEY HAVE TO BUY THE FIELD SO THAT THEY CAN OWN THE TREASURE.

WHAT'S THAT ALL ABOUT, EH?

A wealthy father had two sons. One day the youngest son decided that it was high time that he left home and saw the world.

MEOW, MEOW, MEOW.

What on earth is that meant to mean, Einstein?

YOU TOLD ME TO STICK TO SPEAKING 'CAT LANGUAGE' SO AS NOT TO FREAK OUT THE READERS.

Well, I think that on this occasion we will need to break the rules – otherwise nobody will have a clue what is going on.

WHAT'S NEW?

SORRY. MAYBE I SHOULDN'T HAVE SQUANDERED IT ALL ON WILD AND RECKLESS LIVING.

That's better.

So the cat, I mean the son, got a job working with pigs – which, because he was a Jew, was the worst of the worst. Jews considered pigs as dirty and 'unclean' which means they avoided being anywhere near them and never ate pork.

Marvellous! What a masterly performance from the pair of us.

MASTERLY? WERE WE WATCHING THE SAME THING?

That popular parable is often called the tale of the Prodigal Son. It is all about how much God loves us. Even when we go our own way and turn our backs on God He is always ready to welcome us back with open arms!

BUT NOT TO CHOKE THE LIFE OUT OF US LIKE YOU JUST ABOUT DID.

Should you wish to read the story for yourself in Bible book Luke, chapter 15 and verses 11 to 32 you will discover that not everyone was pleased about the younger son's homecoming. Check it out for yourself.

ARE YOU READY FOR ANOTHER THEATRICAL PRODUCTION FROM MYSELF AND EINSTEIN?

NOT REALLY BUT I SUSPECT YOU'RE GOING TO DO ONE WHETHER WE LIKE IT OR NOT.

Correct! The next parable that we will present to you is entitled 'The Parable of the Wise Builder and the Foolish Builder'. You'll find it in Bible book Matthew, chapter 7 and verses 24 to 27.

The Parable of the Wise Builder and the Foolish Builder

I will play the part of the wise builder and Einstein will be the foolish builder.

THAT WAS PREDICTABLE!

... also decided to build a house but he chose to build it on a foundation of sand. What a silly billy!

To be perfectly honest you couldn't tell the houses apart. From the outside they both looked good. And then it started to rain.

People who allow what God says to go in one ear and out the other are like the foolish man who built on the sand. When difficult times come along they crumble because they don't have a strong foundation.

PROFESSOR BUMBLEBRAIN'S FASCINATING FACTS

Many of the parables that Jesus told were based around everyday things so people understood what He was talking about. Jesus lived in Israel where many people made their living from the land. A story about shepherds and sheep (which is our next parable) would have been right up their street.

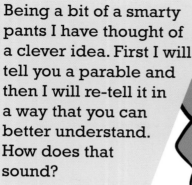

Being a bit of a smarty pants I have thought of a clever idea. First I will tell you a parable and then I will re-tell it in a way that you can better understand. How does that sound?

DON'T RUSH ME, I'LL TELL YOU IN A MINUTE.

Jesus told this parable about a shepherd who had a hundred sheep. One of them strayed from the group and got lost. Without a second thought the shepherd set off to find it. When he found the lost sheep he was over the moon and threw a party to celebrate.

Anyway, here is my up-to-date version of this parable.

Mr Shepherd's class was on a field trip to the farm.

One of his pupils, Shaun Lamb (I trust that you have noticed the clever names I have given the characters) was keen to explore the farm on his own.

While Mr Shepherd led the children around the farm Shaun slipped away to investigate.

But, when it was home time, Mr Shepherd discovered, to his horror, that Shaun was nowhere to be found.

The bus driver was keen to get moving but Mr Shepherd insisted that they wait until the lost lad was found.

After a rather frantic search Shaun was discovered sheepishly (forgive the pun, I can't resist a little bit of humour every now and then) ...

... standing up to his knees in mud in the middle of the pig pen.

Mr Shepherd pulled the lad out of the sticky mud and carried him back to the bus. Shaun's friends were as pleased to see him back safe and sound as he was to see them!

The end.

The Bible says that Jesus only ever said what His Father in heaven wanted Him to say.

Because many of the religious leaders had got used to the sound of their own voice (and had become deaf to God's voice) they didn't like what Jesus had to say, one little bit.

It was pretty obvious that Jesus' parables were His way of showing them how hard they had made it for the Jewish people to live life God's way.

On the other hand the crowds lapped up what Jesus had to say and hung on His every word. They were sick and tired of all the petty rules and regulations the religious leaders forced them to keep. As far as they were concerned Jesus was a breath of fresh air.

WHAT JESUS HAS TO SAY IS AMAZING.

YEAH, AND HE SPEAKS WITH SUCH AUTHORITY AS IF HE REALLY KNOWS WHAT HE'S TALKING ABOUT.

Well, that was short and sweet. So what was the meaning of this mini parable?

SURPRISE ME.

I will.
Jesus was simply saying that if you are one of His followers, don't keep quiet about it. People who are best buddies with Jesus have God's life in them which is like a light. Lights are made to shine so that people can see them and aren't to be hidden away.

This parable was taken from Bible book Mark, chapter 4 and verse 21.

If you were paying attention (and if you weren't I will want to know why) you will remember how I said at the beginning of this book that God's kingdom is anywhere and everywhere that God is allowed to be No. 1.

SOUNDS FAMILIAR.

I also said that God's way of doing things is often very different from ours.

For example, God doesn't just invite the rich and famous to be His friends. The invitation is for absolutely anybody.

So if God isn't picky about who He hangs out with then neither should we be.

I'M NOT PICKY ABOUT EITHER – OTHERWISE I WOULDN'T BE HANGING AROUND HERE STILL.

But first, let me give you a little bit of background to this next story. Jesus had been invited round for dinner at the home of a Pharisee (a Jewish religious leader).

Jesus couldn't help noticing that just about everyone was trying to get the best seats around the dinner table nearest to the host.

The closer you sat to him the more important you felt. Jesus was having none of that 'I'm better than you' malarkey and this is the parable He told to make His point.

You can check out this parable in Bible book Luke, chapter 14 and verses 12 to 14.

The Unforgiving Servant

A king was collecting his debts. One of the king's servants owed him a small fortune which he couldn't pay back. The servant begged to be let off and the merciful king agreed. However, the mean servant refused to let a fellow servant off a small amount of money owed to him.

When the king heard about this he was furious and had the unforgiving servant flung into prison.

What's it about? In the same way that God is forgiving and merciful to us, so He expects us to treat others.
This parable can be found in Bible book Matthew, chapter 18 and verses 21 to 35.

The Faithful Servants

A man was going away for a while so he left his servants in charge of his money. The servants were each given different sums of money to look after. Two of them invested well and doubled their money. The other servant simply buried his pile of cash.

When their master returned he gave the first two a pat on the back for doing a great job with what he'd given them, but he laid into the servant who'd done diddly squat (nothing) with what he'd been given to look after.

What's it about? God gives everyone gifts and abilities that can be used to serve Him. Use them well and they'll do loads of good stuff. But to do nothing with them is a bad idea.

This parable can be found in Bible book Matthew, chapter 25 and verses 14 to 30.

The Lost Coin

A woman had a stash of cash. When some of it went missing did she shrug her shoulders and say 'no worries'? No way! She hunted high and low until she found the missing coin. She was so pleased to have found it that she roped in her neighbours to celebrate with her.

What's it about? We might have gone away from God for a bit and been lost (like the coin) but when we turn back to God there's a party in heaven. This parable can be found in Bible book Luke, chapter 15 and verses 8 to 10.

The Rich Fool

A wealthy farmer was so successful he didn't know where to keep his bumper harvest. He decided to knock down his old barns and build some even bigger ones.

He thought he'd hit the big time and could now put his feet up and live a life of luxury. But that night he died and his selfish life came to a sudden end.

This parable can be found in Bible book Luke, chapter 12 and verses 13 to 21.

What's it about? Don't put your trust in money. Put your trust in God.

Like it or not, sin comes between us and God. And because God is good and pure He can't look at sin. That's just the way it is. But ask God to forgive us and we can be friends again with the God who created us.

Everyone knows that if you do something wrong it's got to be punished. The sin in our lives is no different. But God loves us so much, He decided to allow Jesus to be punished for us. How amazing is that?

When we say a big 'thank You' to Jesus for taking the punishment for our sin and give Him the top slot in our lives, He promises to send His Holy Spirit to live inside us. With God's life on the inside we can then live in the way that Jesus wants us to, just like He taught in the parables.

How good is that?

Jesus used a vine (just like this) to teach us how to stay connected to Him. Jesus said that if we stay joined to Him, just like this branch, we will have a fruitful life.

You can read about it in Bible book John, chapter 15 and verses 1 to 17.

Sometimes we need a spot of pruning from God to get rid of the things that stop us being as fruitful as God wants us to be.

SNIP!

Phew, home at last! That was a close one.

Well, I think that we have just about come to the end of this book on parables.

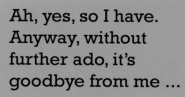

YAWN! YES, YOU'VE TOLD US THAT LOADS OF TIMES, PROFESSOR.

Ah, yes, so I have. Anyway, without further ado, it's goodbye from me ...

It's goodbye from Einstein ...

And it's goodbye from Lightning.

Now where on earth has my trusty tortoise got to?

National Distributors

UK: (and countries not listed below)
CWR, Waverley Abbey House, Waverley Lane, Farnham, Surrey GU9 8EP.
Tel: (01252) 784700 Outside UK (44) 1252 784700 Email: mail@cwr.org.uk

AUSTRALIA: KI Entertainment, Unit 21 317-321 Woodpark Road, Smithfield, New South Wales 2164.
Tel: 1 800 850 777 Fax: 02 9604 3699 Email: sales@kientertainment.com.au

CANADA: David C Cook Distribution Canada, PO Box 98, 55 Woodslee Avenue, Paris,
Ontario N3L 3E5. Tel: 1800 263 2664 Email: sandi.swanson@davidccook.ca

GHANA: Challenge Enterprises of Ghana, PO Box 5723, Accra. Tel: (021) 222437/223249
Fax: (021) 226227 Email: ceg@africaonline.com.gh

HONG KONG: Cross Communications Ltd, 1/F, 562A Nathan Road, Kowloon.
Tel: 2780 1188 Fax: 2770 6229 Email: cross@crosshk.com

INDIA: Crystal Communications, 10-3-18/4/1, East Marredpalli, Secunderabad - 500026, Andhra
Pradesh. Tel/Fax: (040) 27737145 Email: crystal_edwj@rediffmail.com

KENYA: Keswick Books and Gifts Ltd, PO Box 10242-00400, Nairobi.
Tel: (020) 2226047 312639 Email: sales.keswick@africaonline.co.uk

MALAYSIA: Canaanland, No. 25 Jalan PJU 1A/41B, NZX Commercial Centre, Ara Jaya, 47301 Petaling
Jaya, Selangor. Tel: (03) 7885 0540/1/2 Fax: (03) 7885 0545 Email: info@canaanland.com.my

Salvation Publishing and Distribution Sdn Bhd, 23 Jalan SS 2/64, 47300 Petaling Jaya, Selangor.
Tel: (03) 78766411/78766797 Fax: (03) 78757066/78756360 Email: info@salvationbookcentre.com

NEW ZEALAND: KI Entertainment, Unit 21 317-321 Woodpark Road, Smithfield,
New South Wales 2164, Australia. Tel: 0 800 850 777 Fax: +612 9604 3699
Email: sales@kientertainment.com.au

NIGERIA: FBFM, Helen Baugh House, 96 St Finbarr's College Road, Akoka, Lagos.
Tel: (01) 7747429/4700218/825775/827264 Email: fbfm_1@yahoo.com

PHILIPPINES: OMF Literature Inc, 776 Boni Avenue, Mandaluyong City.
Tel: (02) 531 2183 Fax: (02) 531 1960 Email: gloadlaon@omflit.com

SINGAPORE: Alby Commercial Enterprises Pte Ltd, 95 Kallang Avenue #04-00, AIS Industrial Building,
339420. Tel: (65) 629 27238 Fax: (65) 629 27235 Email: marketing@alby.com.sg

SOUTH AFRICA: Struik Christian Media, 1st Floor, Wembley Square II, Solan Street, Gardens, Cape
Town 8001, South Africa Tel: +27 (0)21 460 5400 Fax: +27 (0)23 461 7662
Email: info@struikchristianmedia.co.za

SRI LANKA: Christombu Publications (Pvt) Ltd, Bartleet House, 65 Braybrooke Place, Colombo 2.
Tel: (9411) 2421073/2447665 Email: christombupublications@gmail.com

USA: David C Cook Distribution Canada, PO Box 98, 55 Woodslee Avenue, Paris, Ontario N3L 3E5,
Canada. Tel: 1800 263 2664 Email: sandi.swanson@davidccook.ca

CWR is a Registered Charity - Number 294387
CWR is a Limited Company registered in England - Registration Number 1990308

MORE FROM THE PROFESSOR!

Can I pray? Should I close my eyes? Does God answer prayer? Why say 'Amen'?

For these and other exciting things you always wanted to know about prayer, join Professor Bumblebrain and his expert panel, Einstein and Lightning, in their intrepid investigations. Learn how people prayed in Bible times, why it's so important to pray and how it can change you from the inside-out – as you get to know God more and more!

What are you waiting for? Jump in – and get praying!

Professor Bumblebrain's Bonkers Book on Prayer
by Andy Robb
100-page paperback
197x129mm
ISBN: 978-1-85345-948-1

Other titles in the
series include:

**Professor Bumblebrain's
Bonkers Book on Creation**

**Professor Bumblebrain's
Bonkers Book on Jesus**

**Professor Bumblebrain's
Bonkers on Bible Heroes**

**Professor Bumblebrain's
Bonkers Book on God**

More from Andy Robb!

The Bible is not an easy book to understand if you don't know where to start.

That's why Andy Robb has picked out some of the most exciting stories for you and told them in his own wacky way – which certainly won't leave you bored!

Each story has a cliffhanger ending – and a short Bible passage to look up so you can find out what happened next.

112-page paperbacks, 197x129mm

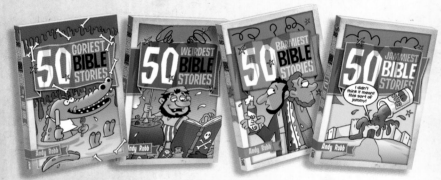

50 Goriest Bible Stories
Cain and Abel, Abraham and Isaac, Moses and his rebellious relations, David and Goliath, Judas and more.
ISBN: 978-1-85345-530-8

50 Weirdest Bible Stories
The Red Sea crossing, Jesus heals a paralysed man, manna in the desert, the dreams of Joseph, Peter walking on water and more.
ISBN: 978-1-85345-489-9

50 Barmiest Bible Stories
How the world began, the adventures of the Israelites, the good and bad kings of Israel, God's mission in sending Jesus to earth and more.
ISBN: 978-1-85345-852-1

50 Jammiest Bible Stories
Jesus heals a blind man, Jesus irks the religious leaders, how the Early Church began, a glimpse into God's ongoing story and more.
ISBN: 978-1-85345-851-4

For current prices visit www.cwr.org.uk/store
Available from CWR or Christian bookshops